Copyright © 2021 Stephany Simmons

All rights reserved.

ISBN: 978-0-578-86684-0

DEDICATION

I dedicate this book to the school-aged Tony Tatum. Because of you, my goal is to bring awareness to children with disabilities and differences that may not have yet been identified as beautiful.

Your story and strength have changed me forever.

ACKNOWLEDGMENTS

Special thanks to Debora Mini for making my visions come to life in this book. You are very talented and I am thankful for your hard work. Thanks for all of those who have supported this work over the last few years. Without your contributions this book would still be sitting on a shelf and unknown to the world.

My name is Morgan, and I am Amazingly Unique! Being unique means, every day when I wake up, just be me.

To be Unique all I have to be is ME!!

Although we share many similarities, out of all the people in the world, there is only one ME!

While you may talk with your voice and words, I've learned how to communicate with my hands. And sign language is super cool, you will soon understand.

I learned that different doesn't mean bad,
that's why I call it unique.

At school, church and in my neighborhood my
friends accept me for me.

But is not always easy being this unique.
When I was new at my school my peers
did not understand

How a person does not always talk with their mouth but mostly their hands.

They thought I could hear if they gave a little shout.

But I was still very lost and confused trying to figure this game out.

But as time went on my friends finally started to see.

They learned when we talked eye contact was key.

Over time my friends became less interested in our difference and loved learning new things about me.

The way I dance,

My funky sense of style

and how I love to draw with my feet!

No matter what I can or cannot do, people love me for me!

But my favorite thing about me will always be that I am
Amazingly Unique!

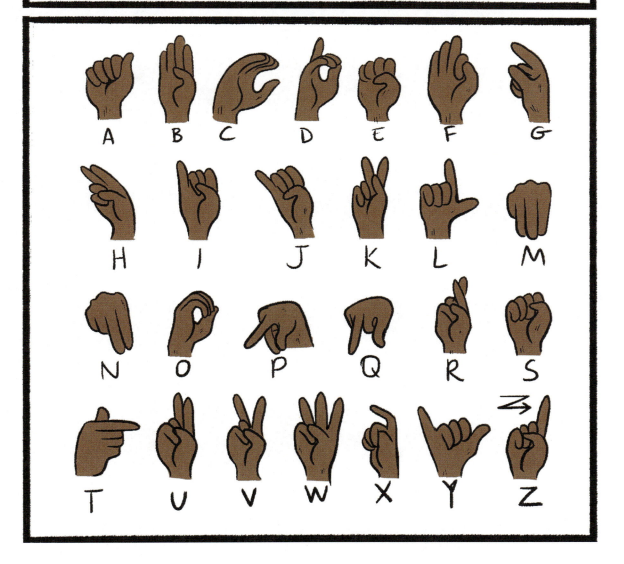

I LOVE YOU	HELP 
MORE 	SAID 

ABOUT THE AUTHOR

Stephany Simmons - First time author and advocate for diversity and inclusion. Stephany is the mother of a young daughter and studying to become a mental health professional specializing in marriage and family therapy.